I0482545

The Art of Drawing Unusual Subjects

Simple Guide Book on Drawing Unique Things!

By Irma Neely

Table of Contents

Disclaimer

While all attempts have been made to verify the information provided in this book, the author does assume any responsibility for errors, omissions, or contrary interpretations of the subject matter contained within. The information provided in this book is for educational and entertainment purposes only. The reader is responsible for his or her own actions and the author does not accept any responsibilities for any liabilities or damages, real or perceived, resulting from the use of this information.

The trademarks that are used are without any consent, and the publication of the trademark is without permission or backing by the trademark owner. All trademarks and brands within this book are for clarifying purposes only and are the owned by the owners themselves, not affiliated with this document.

Introduction

They are impacted by steampunk in their music, as well as in their attire, outline of their instruments, and even the anecdotal personas that they convey with them in front of an audience. Beside steampunk rock, there is rap and hip-bounce music affected by steampunk, and as a rule incorporates a profound however up-beat bass and verses that either delineate the life of a frantic researcher, or a post-prophetically catastrophic world.

Steampunk has been gotten by the craftsmanship culture shockingly quick. You can without much of a stretch discover artistic creations of airships and other flying machines crossing dark skies above tremendous, forlorn scenes. Such craftsmanship can be discovered on the web, at your nearby workmanship shows, and in displays. While the reason and point of view of such artworks is dissimilar to whatever else, the workmanship styles can be fundamentally the same to different styles you have seen. While being dull and dismal, the fine art frequently portrays a vicious ocean, a prison like-lab, or a deadlock world, infrequently Frankenstein-esque. It is anything but difficult to bring up anything steampunk motivated in light of the fact that the style is especially one of a kind contrasted with others.

Attempting to disclose steampunk to some person that has never known about it is extremely troublesome. You may have heard this term now and again and still have no clue what they are alluding to. All things considered, now is your opportunity to learn everything about steampunk that you ever needed to know. Steampunk is a style of cosplay in which the cosplayers dress and talk in certain conduct. To put it plainly, steampunk alludes to a particular type of verifiable fiction.

Regularly steampunk takes a post-whole-world destroying setting in the Victorian period with substantial topics of steam-fueled apparatus. That is a decent general perspective of steampunk, however it can get a considerable measure more included. There are even diverse subgenres of the steampunk cosplay. Steampunk can take the type of Medieval Steampunk, Victorian Era Steampunk, Western Steampunk and that's only the tip of the iceberg!

Today steampunk has discovered its way into pretty much everything. After the film promotion of steampunk we additionally began to see a goad of steampunk realistic books. We even began seeing computer games get the reason. Prominent diversions like "Bioshock" are ridden with steampunk subjects. An enormous number of experts have begun building steampunk themed props. These carport mechanics have transformed pretty much all that we utilize and love into a steampunk thrill.

Genuine steampunk devotees regularly toss meet-ups. This is the place you break out each bit of complex steampunk clothing you possess, even your steampunk sleeve fasteners. You additionally need to catch up on your mid-century language. Dressing the part is one thing, however talking the discussion is an entire other monster. In the event that you have room schedule-wise to dedicate to taking in the language you can have some incredible times. The main downpoint to this way of life is the expense. Most things steampunk don't accompany shoddy stickers. You need to remember basically all that you are purchasing is 100% carefully assembled and unique, so the costs mirror this.

Chapter 1 – How to draw a steampunk bird

STEP 1. Make two shapes, one for the head and another absurd body. Sketch in the one facial rule like so.

STEP 2. Utilizing the aides, draw the body's stream, then attract the little cone-formed bill and in addition the twirl for the bird's expansion eye.

STEP 3. Next, draw the mid-section and start the states of every wing. Include the beautiful outline along the wings' edge like so.

STEP 4. Here you will outline in the plumes which are made of metal. Steampunk articles are produced using every single mechanical part. When the wings are done you can continue to step five.

STEP 5. Attract whatever is left of the body alongside the split tail. Include some trimming the neck and another indented outline idea on the wing's elbow.

STEP 6. You are prepared to complete you're drawing. You should do nothing more than attract whatever remains of the mechanical itemizing on the wings, then draw the really trimming along the center piece of the body. You will likewise include a few spots the bird's brow and additionally along the cheek and neck. Eradicate your slip-ups and you are finished.

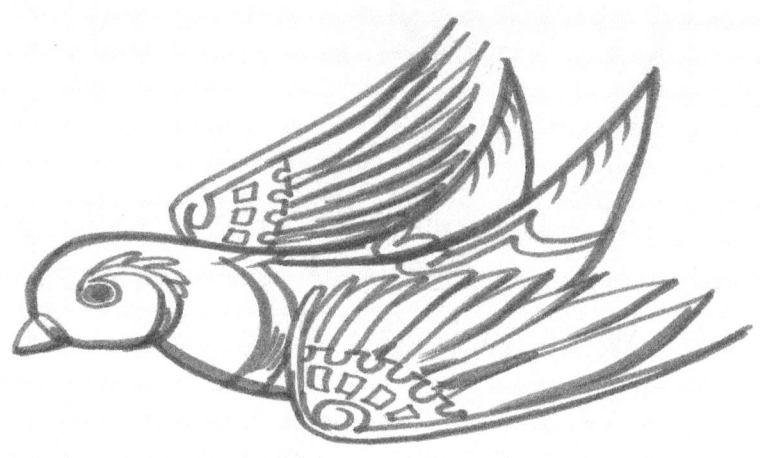

STEP 7. Here is the means by which your steampunk bird looks when you are all done. Presently you can shading the bird in.

Chapter 2 – How to draw a steampunk butterfly

Step 1: Draw the two wings in the 1st step.

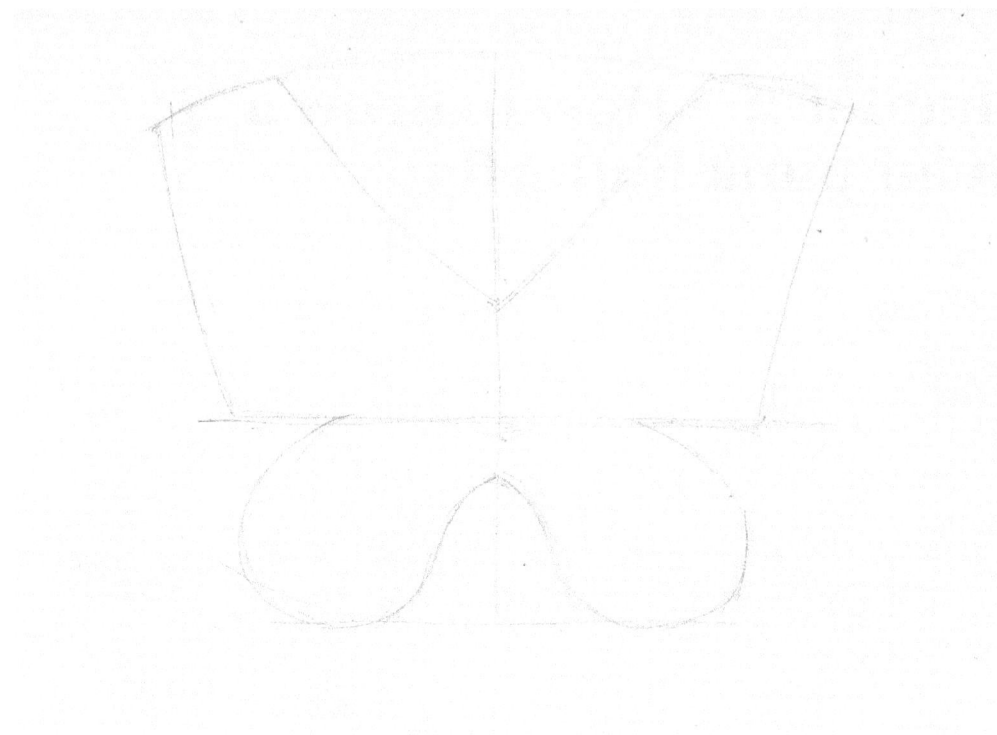

Step 2: Come up with the beautiful shading for those but in a light manner so that we can erase it if needed.

Step 3: now we can work on the face of the butterfly as well as two ears which are above.

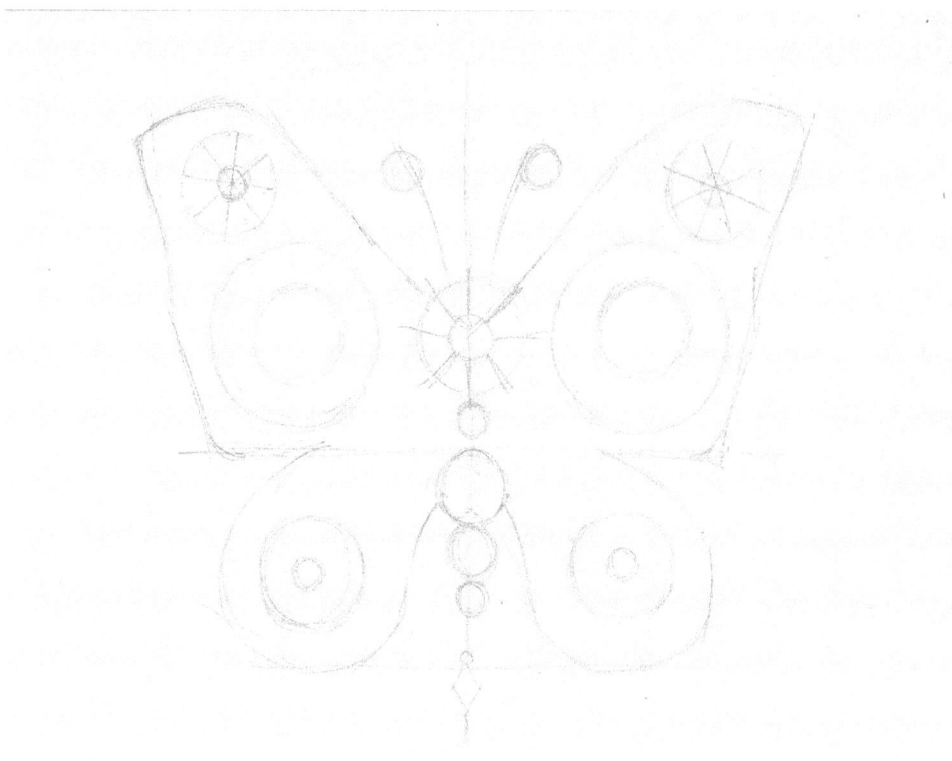

Step 4: Work on the part where the butterfly has its wings to give them a steampunk look.

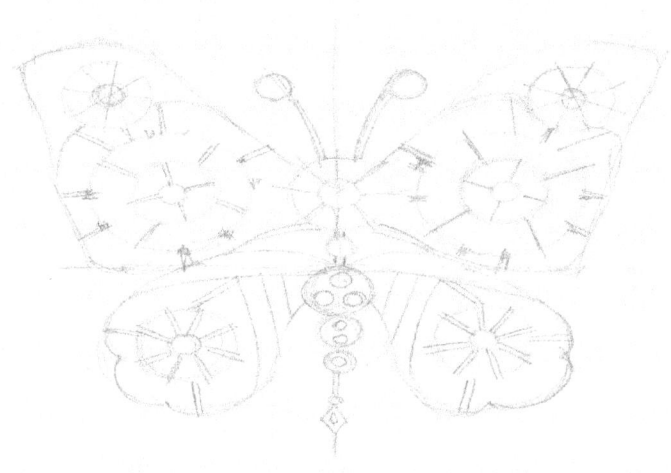

Step 5: lastly you can work on the shading part.

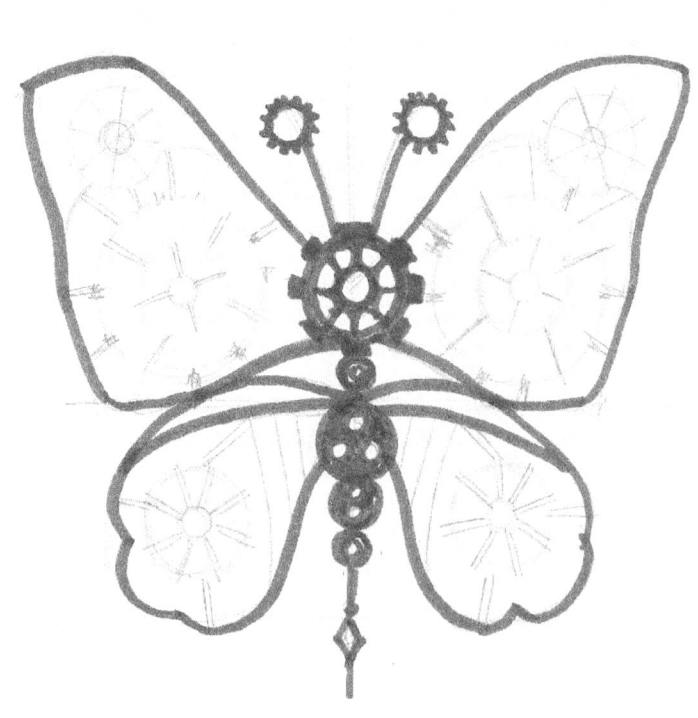

Step 6: After you are done with the main shading work on the final part so that the butterfly comes out bright and awesome.

Chapter 3 – How to draw steampunk face

STEP 1. Portrayal out the shapes for the head and middle like so. You will then portray in the facial rules, then the middle aides also.

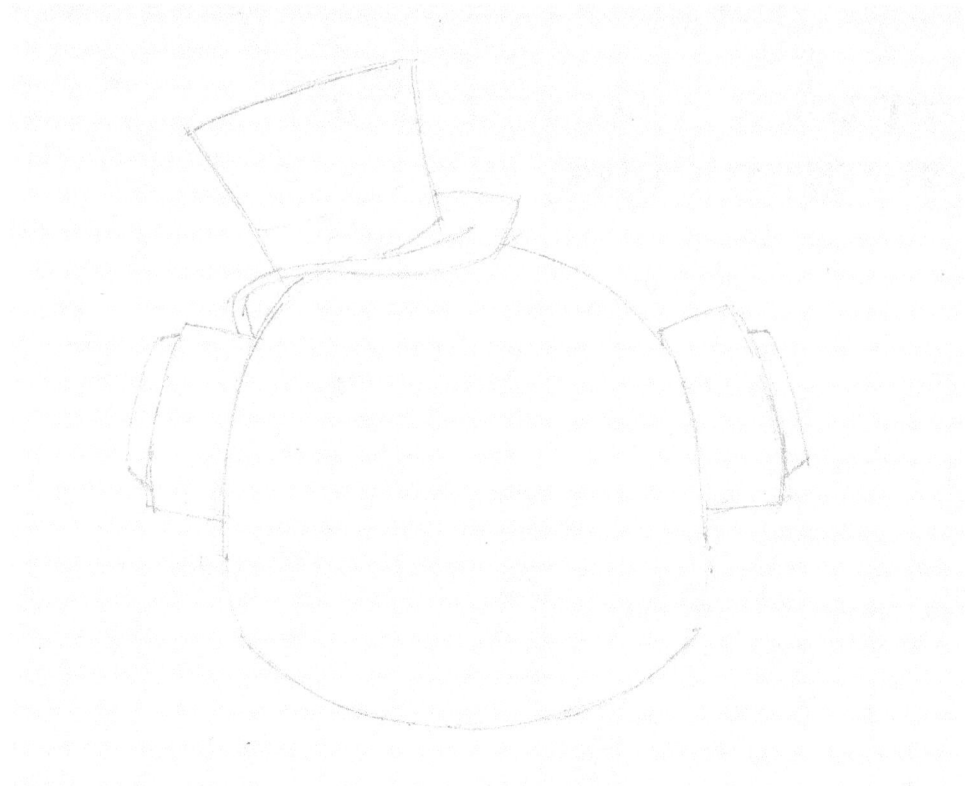

STEP 2. Next, draw the cap's cover and after that draw the circles for every lens from the eye gear.

STEP 3. Sketch in whatever remains of the shape for the material style cap, then draw the strap for the glasses she is wearing on her temple. Sketch in the enumerating to make that dimensional look inside the lenses.

STEP 4. Next, we will take a shot at getting her face shape outlined out like in this way, then attract the wavy short bolts for her hair. You can decide to run with any length or style you like, I picked the shorter bounce.

STEP 5. Presently attract the catty state of her eyes, then attract the lashes, eyebrows, and after that her charming nose and mouth. Add some definition to the eye and mouth zone.

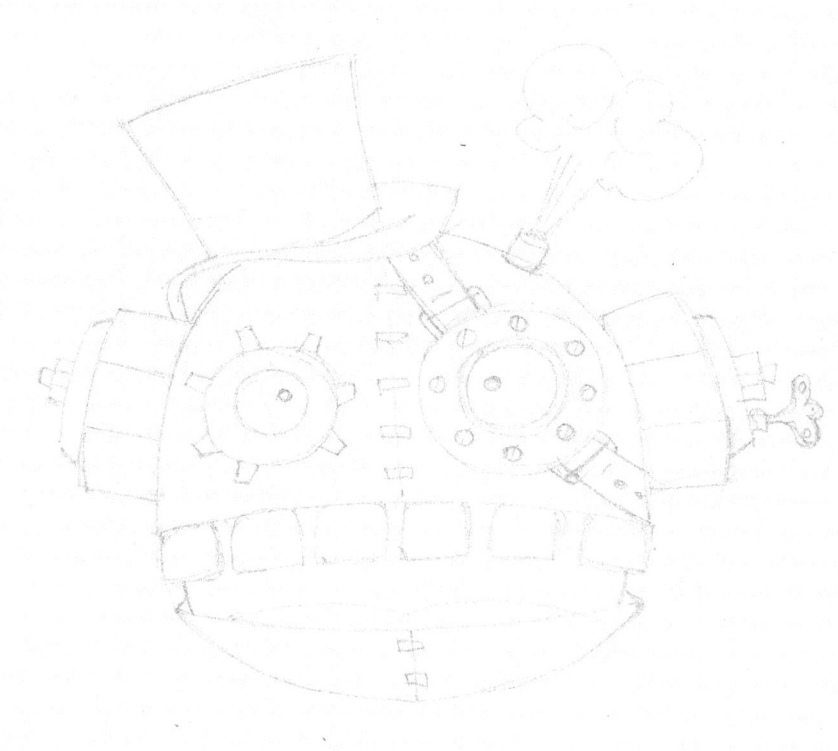

STEP 6. Here you will include the state of her neck, then draw the shirt neckline alongside the span of her bosoms which are secured with the shirt she is wearing. You will be drawing whatever is left of the shirt next.

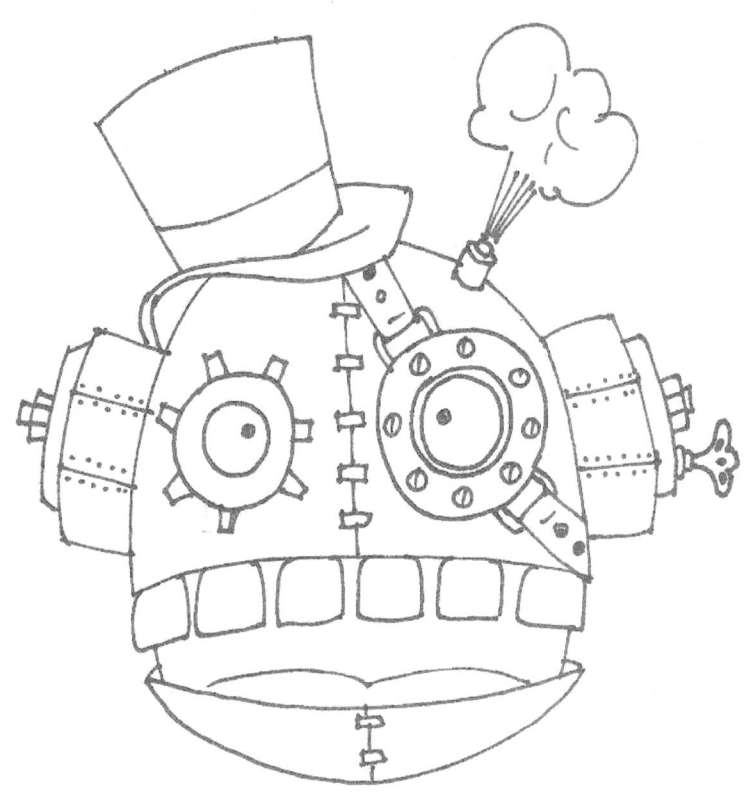

STEP 7. Portrayal out the shoulders, arms or sleeves, then outline in the girdle style vest. Add specifying to her top as wrinkles, wrinkles, and folds. Include the trim in the focal point of her middle which holds the top on decent and cozy. Eradicate your errors and after that you can give up.

STEP 8. Here is the line craftsmanship. Presently you can have a ton of fun shading in your recently drawn steampunk.

Chapter 4 – How to draw a steampunk Owl

Step 1: Draw a vast oval. It ought to be around 2/3 of the tallness of your paper. It doesn't need to be flawless, yet attempt to make it about twice as tall as it is wide, similar to the picture underneath:

Step 2: Make eyes. Draw two circles close to the highest point of the oval, around 1/5 of the range from the top. Draw a littler circle in each, and shading them dark, for the owl's students. Play around with the eyes, in the event that you need—you can make a genuine owl, with in the center straight ahead; an owl drawing so as to take a gander at something, the understudies pointed left or right; or a ridiculous, cross-looked at owl.

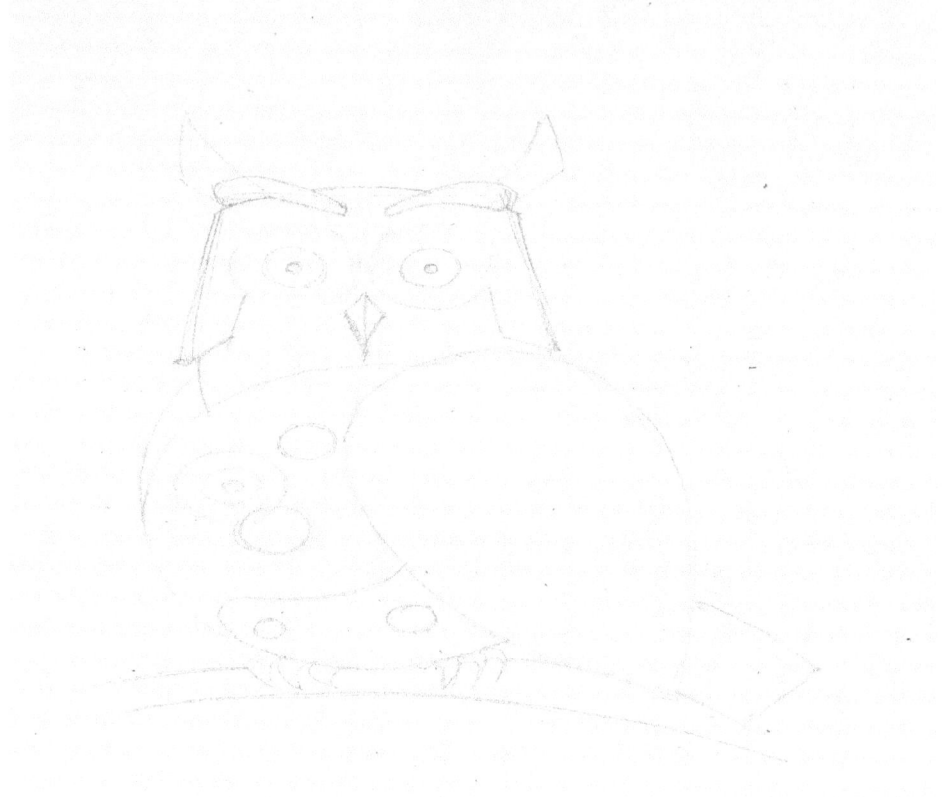

Step 3: Draw horns. Make a wide "V" shape, developing past the oval's edge on both sides, with the V's purpose between the owl's eyes at about their focuses, vertically. The point in the center will give your owl heaps of character. The less pointy the center is, the "more pleasant" the owl will look. The more profound the point, the angrier the owl will show up.

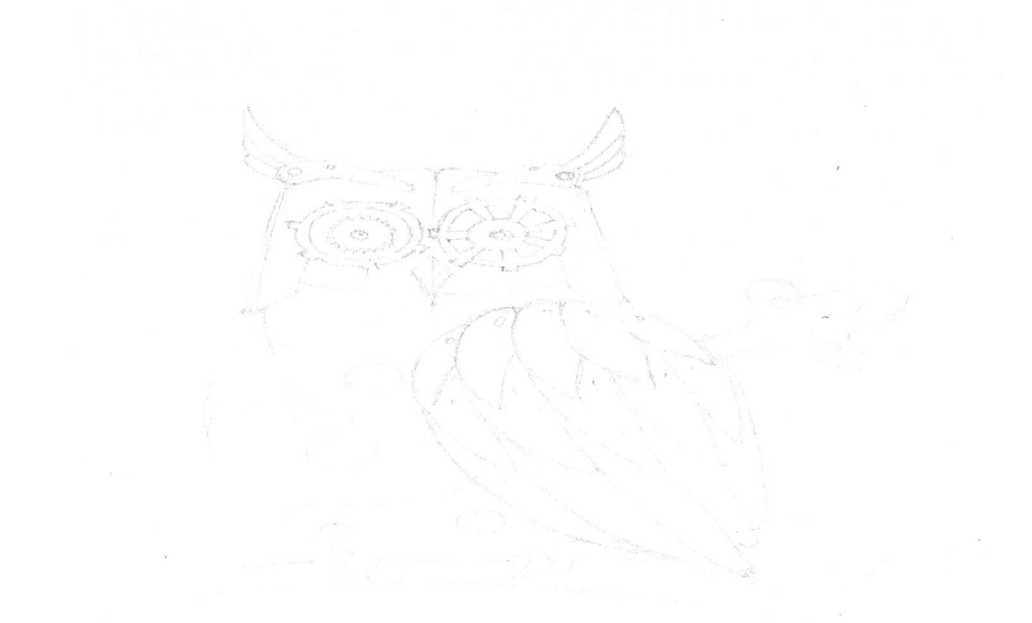

Step 4: Attract the wings. Draw bends from the upper left and right, internal to around 1/4 the oval at the middle, then back outward toward the base.

Step 5: Include claws. Make extended ovals at the base of your owl, three on every side, and after that two level lines for a roost. The roost doesn't need to be impeccably straight—it can look "branchy." Likewise, the claws don't need to be ovals—they can be pointed and sharp, which is particularly great in case you're making a mean owl.

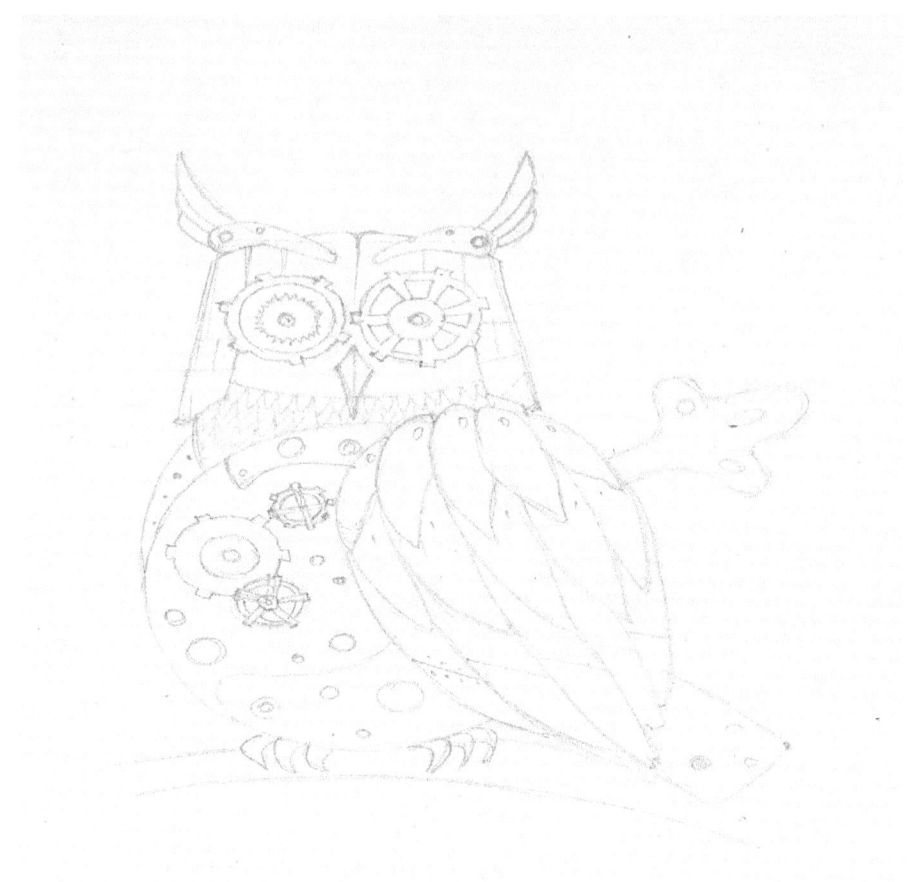

Step 6: Include a bit of feathering. Make little "U" shapes around the range between the "wings" to look like little plumes.

Step 7: Give him the bill. Place a slender "V" marginally lower than the eyes for the owl's bill.

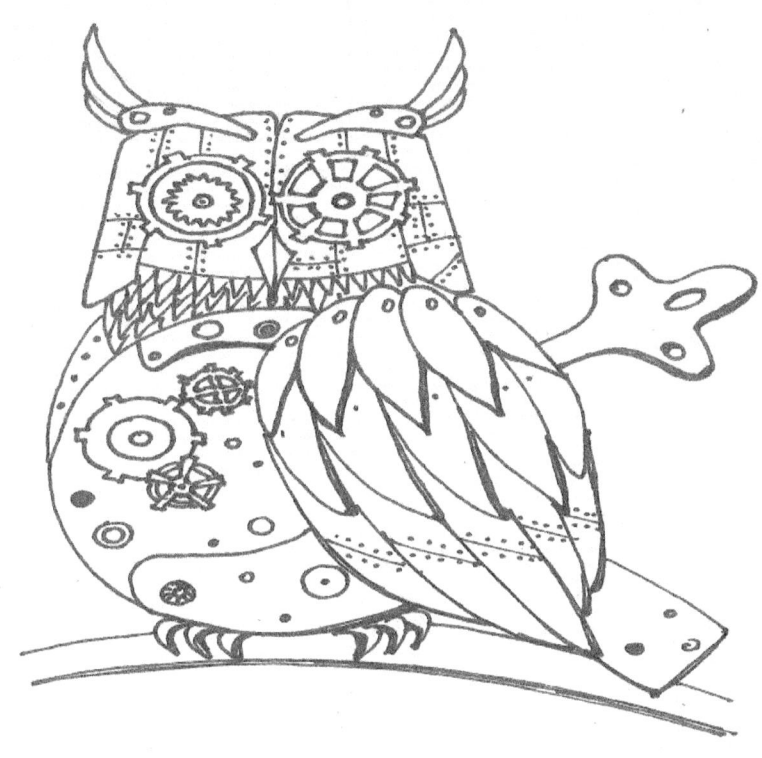

Step 8: Include shading. In the event that you need, shading the "wings" chestnut, and the head and bosom light tan.

Step 9: Get inventive. Include different points of interest as you see fit. You can take after the proposals underneath for including light and shadow, or make up your claim. Since you know how to make an owl, you can make a whole rush of Halloween hooters!

Chapter 5 – How to draw a Steampunk Girl

Step 1

Make an essential line-craftsmanship, I pick SAI Paint devices just to make more less demanding to draw a perfect line-workmanship.

Step 2

Begin fill it with shading utilizing Photoshop, simply piece it with shading, any shading that match with the subject that you need.

At this moment I pick Steampunk topic.

Step 3

This part was so much fun, you can begin exercise with the shading (
Highlight and shadow).

In any case, don't make it to detail, simply put some uncommon point and
do it generally.

Step 4

Last rendering, itemizing, give some dept on it with check and recheck with shine and difference, and so forth …. lastly give some impact on it to with your own particular taste.

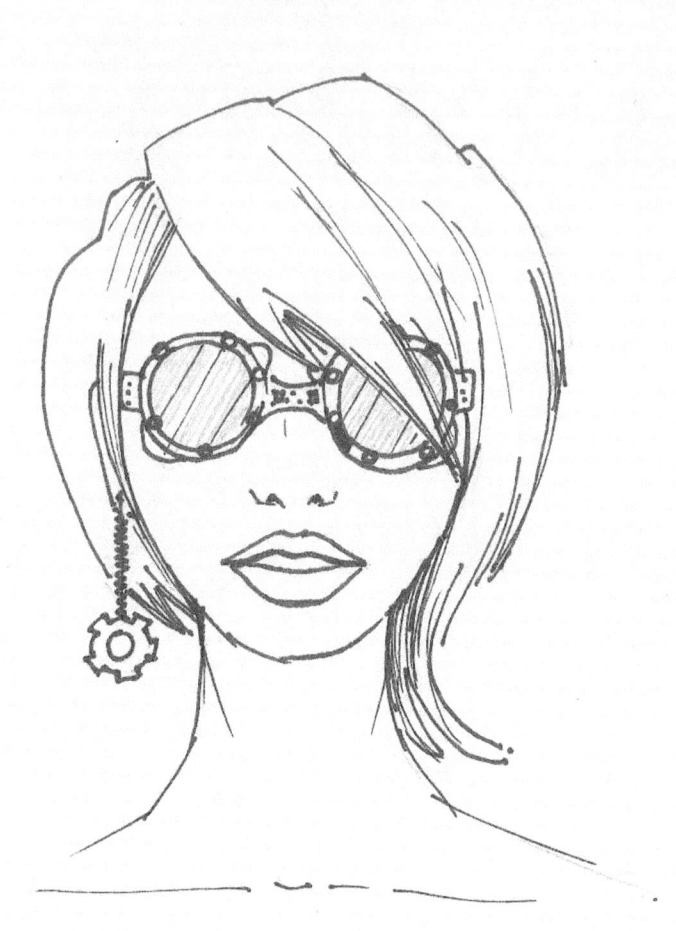

Step 5: Now we can work on her face and the shading part to make her look better and more of a normal human being female.

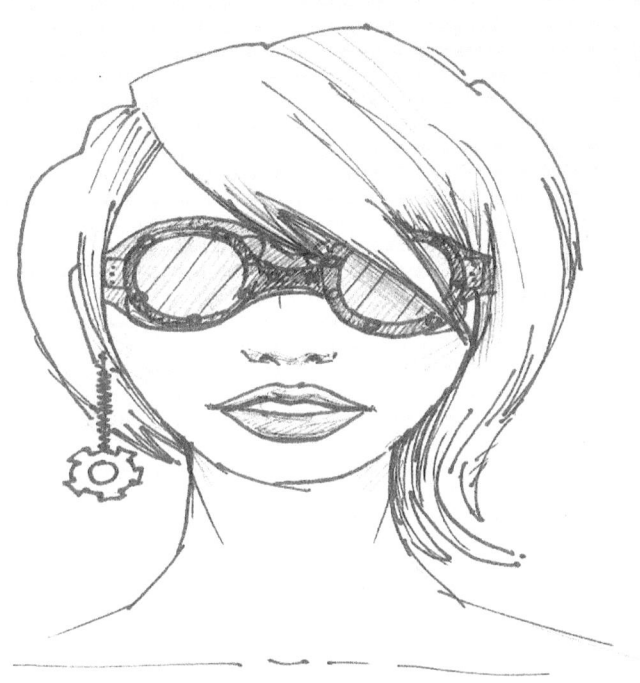

Step 6: Now as you can see in the image above we have worked on the darker shading of the face, so that the glasses and hair give the look.

Chapter 6 – How to draw a steam punk air balloon

Step 1: Open the PicsArt Drawing Tool

Select "Draw" from the principle screen and afterward select "Draw clear" to begin another drawing starting with no outside help. You have the alternative of picking the exact width, tallness, and introduction of your drawing before entering your work space.

Rough Outline

Sketch a harsh diagram of your hot air inflatable with a slight dark brush.
the most effective method to draw a hot air inflatable orderly

Step 2: Final Outline

Diminish the haziness, and in a higher layer follow an exact and clean last diagram. Utilize straight lines and geometric circles for additional exactness. Erase your unique layout.

Step 3: Add Shading

Include another layer and utilize a translucent splash brush to add shading to your inflatable. Just shade one side of your inflatable, the side that is uttermost from the sun.

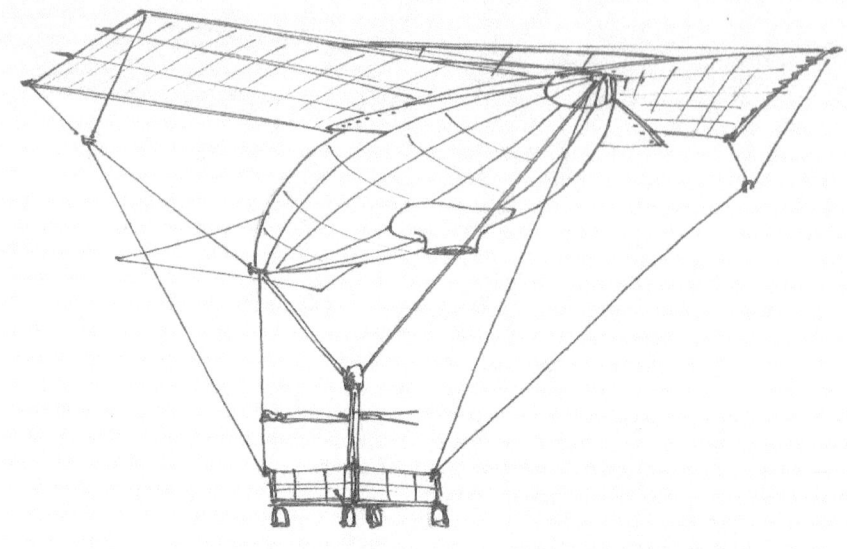

Step 4: Add Color

In another layer beneath your blueprint, add essential shading to you're drawing. Make a point to utilize energizing and merry hues.

Step 5: Add Lighting

Utilize a splendid white translucent splash brush to include lighting in another layer. Add lighting to the zone inverse your shadows, nearest to the sun.

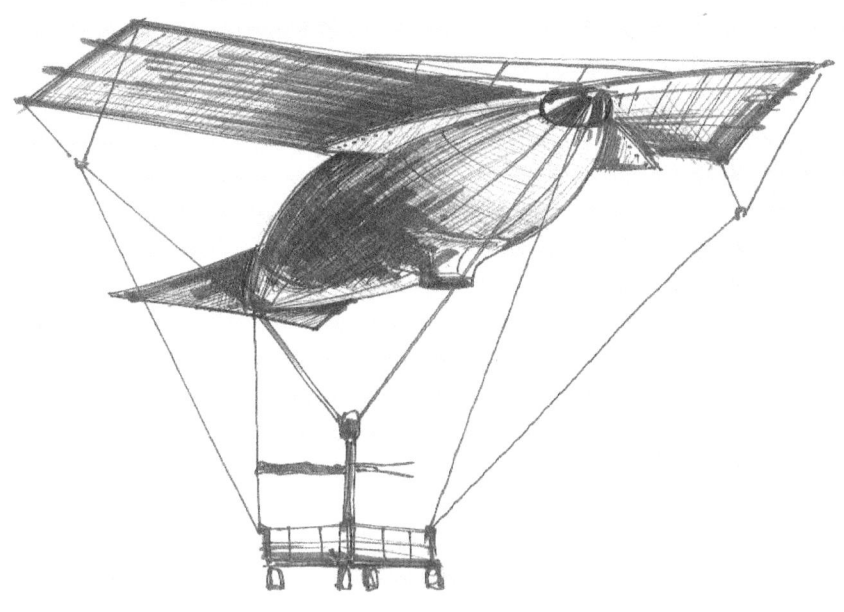

Step 6: Create a Sky

Include a layer of light blue to the foundation of you're drawing. Make mists with a white splash brush in layers on top of and underneath your inflatable diagram and hues to make the figment that your inflatable is truly taking off through the mists!

Conclusion

STEAMPUNK LITERATURE

Steampunk workmanship & outline realizes the nonexistent questions, styles, and innovation of envisioned steampunk universes, in light of a common tasteful of materials, hues, subjects, shapes, themes, and style. With a do-it-without anyone's help state of mind also, accentuation on individual elucidation, the steampunk tasteful shows in each sort of craftsmanship and configuration, including style, furniture, also, devices and in addition the expressive arts. Steampunk creators/craftsmen/tinkerers make and bodge together the old and the new in inventive, shrewd, and lovely ways.

You may have heard this inquisitive expression bandied about in the media as of late, alongside pictures of individuals wearing Victorian garments and outfits, donning all way of surprising frill. You may have pondered internally what the deuce is this?

The term Steampunk started in the 1980's and is utilized to depict a subculture of Science Fiction and Fantasy with an accentuation on option history.

The universes of Steampunk normally concentrate on the period generally known as the Victorian Era with numerous stories set in Britain and America, in spite of the fact that there are various International Adventures and a huge Steampunk following in Japan. Since a large portion of these experiences include all way of peculiar, unordinary and out of date methods of transport, these stories can occur anyplace above, beneath or even inside the world!

Steampunk isn't reflected in any one structure, there are books, realistic books, Jewelry, Fashion, activities and garments. You can frequently discover Steampunk impacts crawling into numerous works of art, and computer games and Role Playing Games.

There are a colossal number of sites devoted to this energizing class, with new locales and fan pages seeming every day. There are likewise various shops which convey a scope of all way of items including Steampunk Jewelry, Quill Pens, USB Drives and Goggles.

Since Steampunk is a genuinely free term, individuals make all way of enrapturing understandings, without a doubt Steampunk can regularly be both an interesting, imaginative and entirely unconventional type.

As of late, the universe of Steampunk has been inching into the standard, through groups like Abney Park, computer games and TV arrangement.

A vast Steampunk affected up and coming discharge is Bioshock Infinity which is a videogame set to ship in 2012. The amusement happens in a city over the mists and conveys numerous unmistakable Steampunk and Dieselpunk impacts.

There are a wide range of translations of the term Steampunk, with diverse individuals contending what falls under this umbrella. Then again, it does appear to be clear that Steampunk was initially begat in the 1980's to characterize a particular sort of writing that was beforehand indistinct. This writing is typically set in, however not bound to, the Victorian time, and combined with advanced developments that may have been imagined amid this time.

Despite the fact that the term Steampunk wasn't begat until the 1980s, its inceptions can be followed back to the nineteenth century with sci-fi sentiment combined books by Jules Verne and H.G Wells. The first TV Series of The Wild West in the 60s was outwardly all that much of the Steampunk classification. Steampunk appears to recommend "What may have been", had our advances in innovation been different; mechanical and steam fueled, maybe without the development of power. Therefore, the symbolism of Steampunk is constantly extremely cutting edge yet at the same time holds the Victorian style - envision metal, wood, glass and a lot of itemizing.

Steampunk itself is not constrained to writing. It has turned into a complete sub society, with Steampunk design, craftsmanship, amusements and even music. What with the fantastical symbolism utilized as a part of Steampunk books, it wouldn't have been long until individuals began to make devices and systems in this style. Individuals have now "steampunked" everything; from telephones to autos, PCs to try and houses! Steampunk dressing itself may not be the most conventional Victorian dress, but rather adds a fun turn to it, utilizing cutting edge and mechanical extras, to make an intriguing and inventive look.

In the most recent couple of years, Steampunk has turned out to be more powerful in standard society. Television Programs, for example, Doctor Who and Warehouse 13 both component Steampunk motivated things, the last having articles planned by Steampunk Artisan Richard Nagy. Justin Bieber even as of late had a feature highlighting metal systems and Steampunk outfits! Steampunk hasn't neglected to impact the regularly developing realistic novel culture either.

Artistic works of mid twentieth Century, and notwithstanding dating to the Victorian period, have affected the class known as Steampunk. While it is for the most part an artistic classification, it is likewise characterized by innovation, for example, steam motors that were fused into the period's sci-fi and dream. It's been depicted as a kind of Victorian-modern, however with more caprice and less vagrants or, as Jess Nevins said, "Steampunk is the thing that happens when Goths find cocoa."

Steampunk has discovered its way into different classifications, for example, sentiment, erotica, and youthful grown-up fiction. Likewise developing in prevalence are Steampunk garments, a line characterized by the unpleasant innovation of the mid 1900's the place a couple of goggles would fit in pleasantly. This individual style incorporates both apparel and gems and, while the garments are not precisely Victorian, including mechanical bits or insights of an a larger number of daring life than a normal Victorian native.

While the class incorporates the Victorian time, it incorporates propelled machines in light of nineteenth century innovation and in addition the otherworldly also and may even happen in a different universe.

Obviously, Steampunk contraptions are coming into this present reality. Individuals have Steampunk'd everything from PCs, work areas, phone, watches and guitars to autos, cruisers, and homes. These items can shift from a grungy look of an overlooked obsolescent to the sparkly exhausted novelty of a Victorian refined man's club. These are metal and copper, glass and finished wood, imprinting and carving, and points of interest for the purpose of subtle elements.

At long last, Steampunk demonstrates a philosophical point too, which is to some degree a blend between the goals of imagination and confidence and the Victorian hopeful perspective without bounds. This last part has prompted allegations that Steampunk incorporates a decent lot of realm love, which is a sensible concern. Another feedback has been that Steampunk concentrates on the best of the past and discreetly clears the issues of the day under the mat.

Steampunk is a sub-classification of punk that is communicated in particular areas, for example, ensemble faires, renaissance faires, Blizzcon, Comic-Con, Halloween, the smoldering man celebration, vast festivals or maybe in a more personal setting with a gathering of companions, on a day outside over a cookout. It is not normally viewed as ordinary apparel, worn on a trek to the shopping center in light of the fact that the vast majorities are new to the idea, and it is less an announcement against particular advanced social patterns, as a declaration of a thought of how things could be totally distinctive.

The Steampunk sort is based around the thought of the continuation of innovation along the confinements of steam force, as though the utilization of fossil fills, and different types of force had never been found. Copper tubing and metal metalwork are viewed as the components most used to develop devices and thingamajigs inside of these impediments. Blown glass and little measures of power can likewise be vital components in making "fiendish gadgets".

Steampunk attire and design is dated around the age where Steam power was most pervasive, so Victorian and Edwardian subjects are a staple when assembling an ensemble

The Steampunk class is dependably generally used to infer an envisioned future where we have come back to steam power because of the consumption of different assets. This thought takes into account low-innovative conceivable outcomes, and is in a few ways greater since it can join cutting edge dream. A couple of steam powered individual wings. Goliath ocean bearing vessels fit as a fiddle of an octopus.

In this manner, "Steampunk" could suggest somebody in today's reality who favors the thought of this other innovation existing over our present situation. Be that as it may, an ensemble can likewise be themed in an advanced sense, delineating an ordinary person who exists in reality as we know it where steam is the most utilized type of force. A charcoal besmudged urchin who lives up to expectations throughout the day in a production line giving steam energy to deliver wonders of advanced steam innovation. An abundance seeker who's weapons are formed from the leftovers of tore separated weapons of war, no more of utilization due to the lack of "old world fossil energizes, however refashioned to store a payload of steam weight with the end goal of dispatching a shot towards anything.

Sketching Drawing - The 3 fundamental contrasts

1. Sketching is generally looser and more liberated

At the point when individuals sketch it is more often than not to deliver a fast interpretation of a scene. This is regularly done in light of the fact that the scene isn't static, for example, a bistro scene with individuals traveling every which way. This kind of liquid, always showing signs of change circumstance, fits a quick way to deal with drawing we allude to as sketching. In this kind of sketching the goal is to get on paper the primary structures and lines of the scene. These lines and structures are regularly straightforward yet lovely in their extremely effortlessness. This type of fast drawing is likened to immaculate observation drawing and obliges a gifted eye and a snappy translation of the smoothness of the evolving scene.

The "detachment" of the lines in such portrays and the virtue of line and structure that gifted craftsmen can accomplish regularly ingrains an incredible vitality into the completed piece.

2. Sketching utilized for reference

Numerous specialists utilize fast portrays to investigate the different qualities and types of a scene for later use as reference material for a more inside and out drawing or painting. These speedy portrayals can be as straightforward or as nitty gritty as the craftsman requires however they are normally not thought to be done pieces in their own privilege; albeit once a craftsman has been made "popular" such outlines regularly get to be profitable. Representation books are a prominent strategy for gathering these sorts of reference portrayals.

3. Drawings and points of interest

A drawing is normally thought to be to a greater extent a completed piece than a portrayal. This by and large implies that a drawing will contain more visual data by method for point of interest and tonal interpretation than a representation. In any case, this is the place the line frequently gets to be obscured; when does a representation turn into a drawing?

Drawings are additionally normally finish articulations of a scene or subject contrasted with the short lived nature of numerous portrayals. Since drawings of liquid scenes, for example, the bistro situation already specified, are not by any stretch of the imagination down to earth the last drawing of such a scene will frequently be done far from the scene i.e. back at the craftsmen studio, utilizing portrayals as reference.

The meaning of a drawing most likely does not mean they are finished with a ruler! Certainly, absolutely structural specialized interpretations are created that way, yet a drawing, whether of building design or not is for the most part done freehand to deliver the affectability and feeling the craftsman wishes to express. Unadulterated building rendering once in a while display aesthetic enthusiasm!